The Art Of Manipulation

Master the Art of Manipulating and
Influencing Human Behavior with Persuasion,
NLP, and Dark Psychology

Jason Miller

COPYRIGHT © 2019 BY JASON MILLER

All rights reserved. No part of this book may be reproduced or used in any manner without the written permission of the copyright owner except for the use of quotations in a book review.

Illustrations Copyright © 2019 by Ralph Williams

Cover photography by Ralph Williams

First Edition: December 2019

Printed in the United States of America

TABLE OF CONTENTS

INTRODUCTION 6

WHAT THIS BOOK HAS TO OFFER? 9

CHAPTER 1: MANIPULATION 16

Manipulation in a Relationship 16

What Is Covert Emotional Manipulation? 19

In-Depth Different Manipulation Techniques 20

How Do You Deal With Emotional Manipulation? 23

How to Spot a Manipulator 27

Early Warning Signs of Psychological and Emotional Manipulation 30

How to Handle Manipulation 33

CHAPTER 2: DARK NLP – PERSUASION 37

Seeking Truth 37

Making a Good First Impression 41

Building Rapport 44

Persuading With Emotion and Pain 52

What Motivates People? 55

Earning the Right to Ask a Question 57

Answering Questions With Questions 58

Softening Statements 59

CHAPTER 3: HOW TO INFLUENCE PEOPLE **65**

Brainwashing 65

Influence People 69

Reciprocity 77

The Pre-Giving Technique 81

Consistency 95

CHAPTER 4: INTRODUCTION TO SOCIAL VALIDATION, LIKING AND SCARCITY **98**

The "Social Proof" Technique 101

Liking 104

Introduction to Authority's Influence 108

Introduction to Scarcity 114

CHAPTER 5: HOW TO TALK	**119**
Words to Use	119
Words Not to Use	123
Probing Questions	124
Zeigarnik Effect	126
Pattern Interrupt	128
Yes Ladder	129
Hypnotic Language Patterns & Embedded Commands	133
CONCLUSION	**142**
ABOUT THE AUTHOR	**147**
REFERENCES	**148**

Introduction

When I was at school, I always wanted to be a public speaker. I didn't know that how difficult it was to be one or how challenging it can be to maintain the reputation of being a public speaker. Still, I went on with the venture and trained to speak in the public. I started with college functions and then went on to take part in debate competitions. I loved the feeling that the hall full of people was attentive to what I was saying to them. It was an amazing experience.

I often wondered how some people wielded magical influence over the rest of the lot. How a bunch of people managed to stay at the top all the time. I idealized the personalities of Martin Luther King and other revolutionaries who enjoyed massive public appeal. When they spoke, people listened to them. What they said to them, they remembered it. What they asked them to do, they abided by. Martin Luther King is no more but still his speech keeps ringing in my ears. I feel inspired and influenced. I want to make it happen what he said in the speech. I want to follow him. Just look at the power of the influence he had exercised and still exercises over the masses.

Incredible is the only word we can give it. These people were inspirations. They used to be massive crowd pullers. The thought crossed my mind more than once how could they manage to make people act on their words? Their power over the masses was just unbelievable. What methods they used? What were the words they chose to speak when they were making calls of action? How they used to dress? What were the books they liked to read? What was their talking style and what gestures were common to them when they talked to a single person and what gestures they made when they used to address a massive crowd? All these questions made a chain and kept spinning in my head while I grew older. In this book, I have taken the liberty to answer all those questions. I want you to know what techniques you can adopt to make yourself a highly influential person. How you can make people to like you? How can you be their leader?

What This Book Has to Offer?

This book carries methods and techniques to make yourself a highly influential person. You can read it, integrate the techniques into your personality and exercise a magnetic influence over the masses. Let's breakdown the chapters of the book and see what they have got for you.

- The first chapter of the book revolves around the topic of manipulation. It carries details on manipulation in a relationship and also the existence of covert emotional manipulation in intimate relations. You will get to learn an in-depth analysis of different manipulation techniques that are used by people. Some of the top techniques are devaluation, gaslighting, lying, projections, targeting victims and playing the victim card. When you move on into the depths of the chapter, you will get to know how you can deal with emotional manipulators. Then you will learn about the techniques to spot a manipulator in your friend circle and in intimate relationships. The chapter also carries details on the early warning signs of psychological manipulation. The chapter ends in telling you how you can handle manipulation like a pro.

- The second chapter of the book focuses on persuasion. You will learn the importance of a good first impression that includes being punctual, being original and also the importance of small talk. The chapter also carries details on how to build your rapport with people. How you can communicate in a better way and how you will be able to set expectations. You will learn how you can be able to persuade people with the help of emotions and pain. Other topics in the chapter include the elements behind motivation of human beings. The chapter ends up in explaining how you can answer questions with the help of questions to ease out the pressure accumulated on your nerves, and also certain softening statements that you can learn to make a perfect impression the people around you. The chapter contains the perfect recipe for being able to persuade the people around you.

- The third chapter spans around the methods that can help you learn how to influence people. This chapter is one of the most important chapters of the book. On the back of the knowledge that you have gained in the first two chapters, this chapter goes on to explain different techniques such as brainwashing technique, the features that matter in influencing others, the principle of reciprocity, the pre-giving technique, the foot-in-the-door technique, low-balling offer, the that's not all technique, and the foot-in-the-door technique. In the end of the chapter, you will get to learn about the principal of consistency.

• The fourth chapter of the book focuses on the importance of social validation in our lives. It explains the importance of social validation, social proof and the principal of liking. Then it goes on to explain the importance of the influence of authority. How authority can be obtained and how it can be exercised to fulfill our obligations and achieve our goals. At the end of the chapter you will find a detailed debate on the topic of scarcity. You will learn how you can be able to play the technique of scarcity and shape people's minds and opinion. Some common techniques include the Limited Number technique, the Deadline technique and the high demand technique.

- The fifth chapter, which also is the last chapter of the book, explains in-depth the methods for how to talk to people to leave a considerable influence over them. You will be able to know what words you should use in order to make an impact. You will also get to know what words you will need to avoid so that the listener may not get annoyed and form a bad opinion of you. Next comes the importance of probing questions and a detailed analysis of the Zeigarnik Effect.

The chapter contains an in-depth analysis of the yes ladder. You will get to know how you will be able to create a ladder by which you will be able to secure yeses from the customer before getting his agreement on the thing you want them to agree. In the example, I have explained how to do that step by step. The chapter also contains certain hypnotic language patterns that people use to leave an impact on the other person. It discusses the importance of hypnotic pacing statements. Then it explains the importance of subtle hypnotic language. After that it explains how to master the art of hypnotic language. The chapter concludes with the topics of the real value and existence of reality and body language that you can use to increase the scope of your influence over people.

This book carries the right recipe to learn how to influence a large number of people. You should take inspiration from the examples in the book and use them to create your own examples. This book doesn't demand that you should have prior knowledge of the subject. You can start right from zero and then go on to learn to be the master of influencing people. Go on and explore the topics in the book. Have a happy read!

Chapter 1: Manipulation

Manipulation is a technique using which a person can indirectly control the behavior, emotions as well as relationships with other people. There are lots of people who get engaged in periodic manipulation. When we tell an acquaintance that we feel fine but in fact we are depressed, it is a form of manipulation because we are on our way to controlling the perceptions of our acquaintances and also their reactions. Manipulation has a deep connection with emotional abuse, especially in intimate relations. The word manipulation is perceived as negative when it tends to harm our emotional, physical and mental health of a person.

Manipulation in a Relationship

Manipulation tends to be highly detrimental for friendly and intimate relationships. If it continues for a while, it leads to poor mental health and in some cases, to the death of a relationship. As far as marriage is concerned, manipulation may lead one partner to feel bullied and worthless. It is a fact that bad relationships have the problem of manipulation, but healthy relationships also give room to manipulation, especially when one partner intentionally manipulate the other to ease out a tense situation, kill the chances of confrontation, and attempt to lift undue burden from the shoulders of the other partner. In many cases, people willingly downplay the element of manipulation to save the relationship. In a relationship, manipulation takes a number of forms such as giving gifts, affection, showing a sense of guilt, exaggeration and passive aggression.

When parents try to manipulate their kids, they may make them feel guilty for one thing or another. Excessive manipulation leads kids to depression, eating disorder, and anxiety or some other mental health issues. A study shows that manipulation in a relationship begets further manipulation. If parents are manipulators, their kids are likely to nurture manipulative behavior. Some signs of manipulation in a parent-kid relationship are absence of accountability, overlooking achievements made by the kids and excessive interference in the life of kids.

In a manipulative relationship, the manipulated partner may attempt to meet up the needs of the other partner at the cost of the needs of his friends or family. Guilt as well as excessive coercion are the means by which a person attempts to secure favors such as a job, a loan or any other material benefit.

What Is Covert Emotional Manipulation?

Covert manipulation happens when a person, hungry for power, decides to have control over you by using deceptive methods to make you change your mind, amend your behavior as well as perceptions. Emotional manipulation takes place under the cover of your conscious awareness and has the power to make you mentally captive. Victims of emotional manipulation cannot sort out what is happening with them because it is just so covert.

A person who is skillful in emotional manipulation, makes you hand over your emotional well-being into his hands. Once you do that, he will feed on your self-esteem until you are devastated.

In-Depth Different Manipulation Techniques

If you say that you are clean of manipulating others, you are telling a white lie. We have to use manipulation at one or the other point in our lives. It can be a lie to ease out a certain situation or just a few sentences of flattery to get a job done. Let's take a look at some common techniques that are used by manipulators.

Lying

Manipulators have one habit in common and that is to lie to other people. They use this weapon to wrong-foot people and to confuse them. Lying is mostly used by psychopaths. Sometimes they opt to keep a certain part of the story hidden in order to put the victim at a disadvantage.

Devaluation

Manipulators deploy the technique of love bombing. They will make you realize that this is going to be the best relationship ever. When you are fully convinced that they truly love you, they will suddenly leave you without any explanation.

Playing the Victim Card

Manipulators often take up the role of a victim for gaining sympathy and compassion from the people who are around them. That's how they can attract you because human beings, by nature, try to get close to the people who are suffering.

They Will Target the Victim

When a manipulator stands exposed in front of people, he tries to accuse the victim to cover up his own wrongdoings. By targeting the victim, he will be able to hide his manipulation.

Gaslighting

Gaslighting is a common technique for manipulating other people. Manipulators ask a variety of questions such as 'You are crazy to say so,' and 'It is in your imagination.' It is perhaps the most insidious technique that sucks at your confidence and the power to feel justified. There are some ways to avoid it and defeat it by grounding yourself in reality and by jotting down things as they had happened. Also, you can open up and discuss it with a close friend. One of the top choices is to contact a support group who can help you recover from this disastrous situation.

Projections

Sometimes manipulators want to blame you for all the bad things that are happening to them. Everyone does that once in a while but psychopaths make it a routine business. Psychologists say that this is a kind of mechanism on the part of psychopaths who want to extricate themselves from the guilt of possessing negative behavior by linking them to someone else's behavior. If you detect anything similar in the behavior of someone close to you, don't shower any compassion on that person. Instead keep a strategic distance from them. (Stillman, n.d)

How Do You Deal With Emotional Manipulation?

There are lots of people around us who are always fabricating a plot to manipulate others by making them feel ashamed of themselves or by snatching their happiness from them if they don't follow their injunctions. Emotional manipulation is quite hurtful for people. Let's see some of the brilliant ways to deal with this problem.

Don't Open up Your Heart in Front of an Emotional Manipulation

People sometimes say, 'I am quite sad to hear that you would think that I forgot your wedding anniversary.' These words make us feel guilty even when we have done nothing to hurt others. There is nothing left to say or apologize to them. You don't have to feel guilty and you should not say anything to those people. The key is not to take care of what they are saying or doing. When you are dealing with an emotional manipulator, you should trust your gut and senses. Manipulators are always looking for a hint and once they find that weak spot, they keep hitting that.

In the above example, you asked the manipulator if he had forgotten your wedding anniversary or remember it? In response to that, they made quite a dramatic scene by putting the guilt on your shoulders for just asking this question.

Emotional Manipulator Is a Always Willing to Help

Some emotional manipulators are always looking for something they can agree to. When you ask them for help, they will take deep sighs to show as if what you are asking them to do doesn't suit them. When you ask them that it doesn't seem like they want to do what you are asking them to, they will turn the tables on you, saying how unreasonable you are for thinking so. If he agrees to do that, hold them accountable for what they do and how they do that. Don't further delve into the details. If you feel that they don't like to do that, ask them to stop. If this is not possible, go take a hot shower or a stroll on a lonely pavement, covered in autumn leaves. Enjoy what nature has to offer. (Harmer, n.d)

Emotional Manipulators Tend to Fight in a Nasty Way

Emotional manipulators like to keep things really nasty. They won't hesitate to backbite you, and also coerce and manipulate others to tell you what they wouldn't have said otherwise. One of the easiest things to note about them is that they won't show active aggression. Instead, they will be highly passive in demonstration of anger. Also, they will create pathways to let you know how unhappy they are with you. For example, they will convince you that they will support for your new job yet when you join and have to consume lots of time on office work such as creating power point presentations and charts or graphs, and get busy as a beaver in the work, they will play loud music in the home or watch TV late at night. If you dare ask them about the reason for this behavior, they will go on with their excuses and say you just cannot expect life to stop. They can be so much annoying to say the least that at times, you will want to strangle them that will land you in jail.

How to Spot a Manipulator

It feels like hell to be emotionally manipulated. Emotional manipulation is considered as highly destructive, which is why it is vital that you know how to recognize a manipulator in your life. The feat is not as easy as you might think because manipulators are skilful in what they doing. Gradually, as they see positive results, they will keep raising the stakes over time. They will be doing their job and you won't even realize what is happening. If you know the signs of an emotional manipulator, you can easily detect them around you.

They Will Play With Your Grasp of Reality

Emotional manipulators are skilled individuals when it comes to crafting lies. They will make you realize that something didn't happen when in reality it had happened. They attempt to influence our sense of reality. They are so good at doing that they we end up questioning our own selves whether what they are saying is right. In fact, we start doubting our own sense of reality that ultimately causes confusion. If you spot someone attempting to change your perception of reality, you should insist that it all sits in their imagination, and that it has nothing to do with reality. Don't let it overcome your senses.

They Will Play the Victim Card

Emotional manipulators can be easily detected because of the fact that they attempt to play the victim card more often. Whatever is becoming wrong in their life, they try to blame it on someone else. One or the other person finds himself in hot water when manipulators get caught up in an incident, because they start complaining that they have been wronged. They think that if they are unable to do a job, it is someone else's fault for setting high expectations.

They Will Not Hesitate to Hit at Your Weak Spots

Emotional manipulators always know about your weak spots and they won't stay back to push them when they get an opportunity to do that. For example, if you are worried about losing your hair, they will pass a comment on it in front of strangers or the girl you want to marry. If you are insecure about your color, they will not hold back on discussing the same in front of everyone. If you have to prepare a project to present at the office, they will try to discourage you and intimidate you by pointing out how the participants will judge you and question you. That's how they can shake your confidence and make you feel bad about the other day.

Early Warning Signs of Psychological and Emotional Manipulation

Psychological manipulation is done through mental distortion as well as emotional manipulation in order to seize power and gain privileges at the expense of the mental peace of the victim. Here are some tricks that manipulative people keep up their sleeves for coercing others and push them into a disadvantageous position. There is a difference between habits and manipulation, but it is you who must be able to recognize it.

When someone is trying to manipulate you, he will try to make you speak first. He will try to ask you inquisitive questions that would establish a baseline about how you think or behave. This helps them evaluate your strengths as well as weaknesses. If someone is asking too much questions that you find properly crafted and planned first, you are being targeted as the speaker might have a hidden agenda for doing that. This kind of psychological manipulation can happen in an intimate relationship or at the workplace with a colleague. The best course to take is to listen to them, check their behavior, and answer well-thought replies until you are able to tell if the person is doing that intentionally or by habit.

People also try to manipulate you by intellectual bullying as well. Some people consume considerable time on collecting facts and figures about a number of things in order to be an expert. Also, they want to be more knowledgeable in different areas. In fact, they want to show everyone that they are the experts in a certain field or more than one field. Not bad if they have studied hard and authentic facts, but the problem is that they advocate alleged statistics and facts, and also incorporate other data in their speech that is alien to you. They attempt to download from their brain such information that you don't have access to. If they are doing that for educating you, you will know from gestures and expressions. Manipulators hope that they are able to impose their agendas on you. By exhibiting themselves as experts, they will use this technique for no other reason than to make you feel inferior, unsettle you, and then use you for their personal benefits.

People at the helm of affairs in the government sector and the corporate sector love to entangle people into a web of paperwork and red tape. They use their position to manipulate others into submitting to something they dislike. Bureaucrats also use their influence to delay any kind of fact finding into their wrongdoings in the office.

How to Handle Manipulation

Manipulators can be your parents, intimate partners or even kids. There is no solid definition of a manipulator which makes it hard to handle. You can tell that you are being manipulated if you are losing power in a relationship, and also when conflicts are replete with emotional factors.

The first principle to deal with a manipulative person is to feel safe in a relationship. If you are not feeling safe anymore, you ought to develop a plan for maintenance of your health. You need to find a person whom you can trust and who is there to listen to your explanations. If an intimate relationship is failing in making you safe, you should remove yourself from that environment temporarily or even permanently if things don't appear to be coming back on track. Tell your intimate partner or a family member that you will not tolerate their screams and that you will not come back to their home until they stop shouting at you. Try out the following things:

1. Lock your door to cut off communication.

2. Get yourself out of the apartment.

3. Stop the car if you are driving and he is shouting at you unendingly.

4. Refuse to accompany that person in the car.

5. Pack up and leave the apartment to live in a hotel or with a friend.

You should wait for the right time to talk if you must initiate a conversation with the person who is manipulating you. When you think that the boundaries have been crossed, you should freeze for a moment to decide on the limits once again. You may choose not to escalate a tiny argument into a big one.

When your partner feels rejected, it is not the right time to initiate a conversation. If you are ready to confront the manipulator but you also know that the person is vulnerable to your threats such as leaving the apartment, you should wait for the right time to initiate the discussion. Confront them when they are in the state of listening. Then expose them. If the manipulator happens to be one of your parent, you should walk cautiously. Don't do anything in haste. Usually parents are not expecting this kind of behavior from their kids that's why you have to keep the tone of voice moderate.

Especially if they aged, they won't be able to sustain any aggression. Speak with reasoning.

Another top tactic to handle manipulators is to take a non-combative approach for fighting back whenever you get attacked. You cannot take out anything productive by arguing so give your partner time to speak. Listen to them in a calm state and try to absorb what they are saying, and then react to it in a sensible and calculated manner. It is not easy to state your point of view when the other person is making exaggerations or exhibiting emotional intensity. Amidst all this remember one thing that you can always say a big 'No' to something you don't approve of.

Chapter 2: Dark NLP – Persuasion

The basic idea behind the development and study of Dark NLP is that people don't have any concrete identity and they have a lot of characters to take up. Dark NLP means that the fluidity of identity of a person offers a gateway for manipulators. This fluidity pushes them to adopt a personality that manipulators are looking for. They start behaving as per the will of others. This pushes them into a circle of malicious influence by manipulators who use their dark spells on them.

Seeking Truth

Stoicism has a few central teachings such as it reminds us about how unpredictable our world can be and how short time span our life has. How we can be strong and how we can take control of ourselves are the questions that everyone needs answers to. It deals with perhaps the greatest problem of our life that is the absence of logic. We usually get carried away with the flow of our impulsive behavior that entertains our senses rather than logical reasoning.

Stoicism is different from the other schools of thought in that it is practical and is not concerned with just our intellectual faculties. To succeed in the world, we must be able to do things that we would not have done in normal situations. Most of us don't try to do things that they should be doing in order to succeed in life perhaps due to the fear of unknown.

Most people trust things as they are appearing to their eyes without realizing the fact that the reality can be way more different. We should be seeing things in our surrounding as they would be, had we not been there. Our surroundings demand that we focus on what feel they are giving off such as how they are looking. The effect the sun light or the artificial light has on those surroundings can be a subject to study. You should closely observe the movement, the animals and the landscape of the place you are in. Notice the soundscape of the area.

When you are able to keep your focus on this, you will observe that a unique sense of simplicity will arise out of it. Things will appear to be more poignant. Try to disconnect from your surroundings to see the real form of things. Most people have formed a habit of looking at their surroundings through the lens of how it is going to affect them. This affects our judgment of things. We try to form a connection of things to our lives to assess whether they will fit in or not in our lives. For example, a luxury car belonging to a person will make you realize that you don't own one. When a person is taking off a holiday, it will make you realize that you don't have a holiday. That's a self-centered and self-referential lens. You should better avoid that to see the truth behind things.

The problem behind why we don't see the truth is that we don't want to see things as they are. Short glimpses of things as they are, are always there for you. All you need is to disentangle yourself from your own self and then see things as they ought to be. In simple words, we should be objective when observing our surroundings. Subjectivity colors our judgment and we can only see things in relation to how they are affecting us and not how they, in reality, are.

When we adopt this attitude, we are able to see things in a broader perspective. Every scene we will see will carry a unique signature and a unique identity to express. Even a parking lot has a unique identity to offer if you don't see it as a space for your car to stay for a while. This practice can be applied to the people around you. Notice them as if they don't have any connection with you and you will see their true self.

Making a Good First Impression

When we meet someone, it takes a few seconds to judge his personality and evaluate him. You will form an opinion of him and the other person is also doing the same during the time of your meeting. We forget the latter part most of the time. He will take notice of the dress that you are wearing, your gestures, your mannerisms, and also the way you have done your hair. Each day we meet new people who try to evaluate us and form impressions of our personalities. There is a common saying that the first impression is the last impression. It is a truth because once a person has concluded the process of calculating the first impression of your personality, he is unlikely to alter it or reverse it. Without a doubt the first impression sets the tone for the relationship. Thankfully, we can learn some smart techniques to create a brilliant first impression.

Be Punctual

You are on your way to inking a business deal and you have to meet your business partner for the first time in a hotel. If you make an excuse that you are going to be half an hour late, the other person is not going to be interested in your excuse for getting late. Even if he waits for you and finally signs a deal, he will have it in his heart that you are not a reliable person. Schedule your time as such to reach a few minutes earlier than expected. You should keep in mind the possible delays such as a traffic jam, and work on it to cut down on delays and be on time for the meeting. (Making a Great First Impression, n.d)

Be Original

Making a good first impression means that you ought to blend in with the other person for a while. It doesn't mean to lose yourself or pretend to adopt a fake personality. The best possible way to make a lasting impression is to be yourself in front of the person you are meeting for the first time. In this way you will not have to wear a fake persona each time you meet him. You will feel more confident, build solid trust and also earn respect as well as integrity from your partners.

Small Talk

If you don't open communication with the other person, it is impossible to create an impression. What topic you choose for small talk, what tone you are using, what words you select to express your thoughts matter a lot when it comes to starting a conversation. Take a couple of minutes to learn about the person. Talk more about his interests and likings. Try to know him. (Making a Great First Impression, n.d)

Building Rapport

Rapport is generally a two-way connection between different people and it must stay so. It is not something you can create yourself. In fact, you can learn how to stimulate it by following some simple steps. The very first thing to look after when you are trying to build a rapport is to give a check to your own appearance. It will help you form a connection with people. It must create a barrier. You can choose a dress that is slightly better than the dress that the other people are wearing. You should go for a modern dressing arrangement. If you think that you have excessive dress layers, remove some clothes to suit the situation. You won't want to be the butt of all the jokes cracked in a party.

Some Basics to Take Into Consideration

When you are communicating with someone, you should keep in mind the following basic elements.

- You need to express yourself as culturally appropriate. Criticizing a particular culture or talking too much about cultural taboos will present your persona as a culturally inappropriate person that is not good for business and other social matters as well.

- You should wear a smile on your face when you are communicating with the other person.

- One important thing to keep in mind is to remember the other person's name when you are communicating with him. It helps you build up a more personalized approach toward them. This brings us to Dale Carnegie's best seller book 'How to win friends and influence people.' Carbine argues that the key to win the hearts of the other people is to remember their names and then addressing them by the name when you meet them in future.

- When you are talking to someone, you should hold your head in an upright position and also maintain a good and confident posture.

- The key to building a good rapport is listening carefully to what others are saying to you. You should be attentive to the minutest of the details they are trying to discuss with you.

- The most amazing thing is not to overstay your welcome at any place you go. Don't let others get fed up with your presence.

Elements of Communication

There are three different elements of communication to make a killer first impression. Let's analyze them.

Mirroring: The first of all in Natural Language Processing technique is mirroring. This suggests that a person's behavior should match that of the others so that there should be no barrier in the communication. When the other person doesn't remain comfortable in talking to us because our behavior is making him reluctant, a communication gap is a must to build up. Mirroring helps us overcome such barriers.

Controlling the flow of conversation: This is yet another important element in conversation. We have to learn to control the flow of our conversation. It is not anything such as dictating other people or simply overpowering them in the conversation. The main objective is to fully engage the listener into what you are talking about. It doesn't mean that you start being coercive in the communication, but instead you should be able to engage the other person into the idea that you are trying to download from your brain.

Setting expectations: Once I met a client to ink a business deal. We had a good chat in the half-an-hour meeting that we had. The next day I texted her to inquire about a missing point in the proposal and to know whether she wanted me to include it and email her the updated proposal. I expected her to respond in ten minutes but she didn't reply until I sent a second text around eight hours later. During those eight hours I kept thinking if that person liked me or not or if she was considering my proposal or not. I had set wrong expectations and this kept me on the edge. We should set expectations to the minimum and as natural and logical as we can whenever we see a new person. This is minimize undue pressure on our nerves.

How to Set Expectations

This section contains a short step by step guide on exactly how you can set expectations in any conversation. The very first step is to understand that it is very hard to set and then fulfill expectations. You should be able to verbally articulate or write on a piece of paper about the expectations you have for the other person. The next step is to know when you should set expectations such as the time during the conversation when you need that. How to communicate or when to communicate them?

You need to help people see the bigger picture. They should know the 'why' factor behind the expectations that you are trying to set. When they understand the reason behind setting expectations, they are likely to fulfill them. For example, you are expecting them to finish a job in a thirty minutes timespan. You should tell them why it is important to finish the job in a short window of time. Once they know the 'why' factor, you have successfully set the right expectations.

When you are done with the initial steps of setting expectations, you should move on to have a couple of meetings with the other person to discuss about the expectations that you have set to know whether they are on schedule or not and also how they are approaching the said project.

You should be regularly conversing with whom you have set your expectations. They may have expectations from you. The ideal scenario is that both of you get your expectations fulfilled. Better for business and long-term commitment.

It is always a good idea to bring your expectations into written form as written things offer us greater clarity. Unwritten things are dependent on our memory that's why chances are high that we may forget them.

The last step is to get agreement from the other person that he will fulfill his expectations. Also, give your agreement to the other person that you will fulfill all the expectations that the other person has set for you. This kind of mutual understanding will boost up confidence in your relationship.

Expectations can be set and fulfilled by mutual agreement. Usually, we fail in communicating what we expect from others in a lucid way. This ambiguity takes its toll on our relationship. When the ambiguity is completely removed, the next step is to stay committed to what you have agreed upon. This builds up the base for a long-term relationship. Good for business!

Persuading With Emotion and Pain

The most prevalent behavior among people is that decisions should be based on logic. We love to be rational because we think this kind of behavior will help us succeed in life, but we forget along the way how much power emotional persuasion has. There are particular emotions that help in persuasion. On top of all of them is sadness. It is a kind of emotional pain that is characterized by the feelings of loss, helplessness, sorrow and disadvantage.

Sadness slows down the pace of decision-making. It creates a fog in your brain and compels you to make decisions that are viable only for a short-term. In addition, sad people are spontaneously drawn toward happiness. If you have the ability to appeal to their sadness, you can persuade them and influence their decisions.

Anger is another emotion that you can use to persuade people. It can be defined as an intense emotional response. It suggests that the basic boundaries of a person have been violated. Latest studies suggest that angry people are more capable of analyzing things and also distinguish between weak and powerful arguments. In the moment of anger, you are more in control of things, experts believe. If the amount of stress is reasonable, it will give a major boost to your optimism.

If you take a look at different marketing campaigns, you will know how business strategists are using these emotions to persuade people into buying their products. When you appeal to a person's emotions, you are on your way to creating a lasting connection with them that brings them in the perfect state to respond to your calls to action. When the connection has been established, they can understand what you are trying to convey to them, and they will accept it as well.

You should understand how it is working on you. Analyze a couple of businesses and charities and see what emotions they stir up inside you. Think of the ad of a company that provides controlling services for roach infestation in houses. Think about the picture of a roach getting killed by an employee from the pest control company. What emotions does this billboard stir up in you? It should be a combination of anger, anxiety and happiness. You get angry and anxious because you recall how much destruction these roaches have brought to your home, but finally you become happy that the pest control company is going to get rid of it. This will compel you to follow their call to action. You are easily persuaded when the marketing campaign played with your emotions.

What Motivates People?

Active listening is a skill that you can acquire and also develop with untiring practice, but most of the time it is a difficult skill to master as it takes considerable patience and time. Active listening means that you should fully concentrate on what is being said to you instead of just hearing what the speaker is saying. It involves use of all your senses. You can show the speaker that you are an active listener with the help of verbal as well as non-verbal messages. The most common gestures are eye contact, smiling, nodding and saying yes or no in order to encourage them to continue. There are different gestures and signs that show that a person is actively listening to what is being said.

Smile: some people express their tendency to actively listen to the speaker by passing slight smiles off and on. You can pair up your smile with the nod of your head to make them more meaningful.

Eye contact: if you are looking to the sides, the speaker will take it as a non-attentive gesture. Eye contact is a must to show the speaker that you are actively listening to him. However, in some cases, eye contact can be intimidating for a shy speaker. You have to determine how much eye contact you need to make an impact. For leaving a healthy influence, you should add a couple of smiles to the eye contact.

Posture: your posture tells a great deal of details about your personality and habits. Attentive listeners develop the habit of leaning forward while they are listening. Active listeners also tend to give a slant to their heads.

Earning the Right to Ask a Question

Have you ever wondered how a salesman sell products to a big number of people? He carries solutions to the problems of people. Selling is not about convincing people into purchasing a product. Instead, it is about tracking down what people want and then providing them with the same. It is about helping people manage their lives in a better way. When an entrepreneur is producing a product, he has to keep certain questions in his brain. He has to ask the right questions from himself. If you don't ask the right questions, you don't know what the needs of the buyers are and how you can fulfill them.

Answering Questions With Questions

If we talk in general, people don't like a question in response to a question as an answer. But doing that has significant advantages. Perhaps one of the best feelings is that it relieves the pressure off your back and diverts it to the one who is asking the question in the first place. It helps because as long as you have to answer questions, you will be on the defensive side and you will have to feel the discomfort attached to answering questions. By throwing a question in response of a question, you will push others into the same situation in which they gave pushed you earlier on. Some questions are less a question and more an attack on the listener to unsettle him. This method is the best to take the heat off of you and channelized to the speaker. This method will also help you set the tone and the temperature of the conversation you are having with the other person. If you are answering a question with a question in response, you are on your way to get an answer that you would otherwise not have achieved. This is how you can get yourself out of stick situations by answer tough questions with questions.

Softening Statements

This section highlights how to soften your harsh statements or questions using a simple technique. One day I rushed to a bank to pay my bills as I had to take a flight to Los Angeles where my daughter and wife waited for my arrival. We had planned a vacation together. The line at the billing counter was a pretty long one. I broke the line and approach the cashier while a woman, who had been there for quite some time, stood there and saw what I was doing to her. She waited for a full minute before shouting at me and asking me what I was doing. "What do you think you are doing young man?" she almost shrieked into my ears. I took a glance around me to see who she was and why she was shouting at me. It was then that I realize that I had broken the line. When I heard the shout, I got mad and I really wanted to do the same to her, but I held back and asked the cashier to help her first. This really calmed her down and her anger vanished into thin air in a matter of seconds. She was an old woman. I realized that I would be in her place someday. Yelling is normal to many households. I grew up in the house of yellers. My parents and siblings loved to do that and it was not always done in anger. Yelling refers to the tone of our voice, but a sharp sound appears to be really harsh and brash. I got used to it as I spent around twenty years listening to this.

I had married to a calm and peaceful girl who would loved to convey her messages in a polite tone. Kirstin was a beautiful lady who would calm me down whenever I happened to burst out in anger. She advised me to lower down my voice tone whenever I was in anger. She believed that a calmer tone really helps in settling down a hyper situation. That day in the bank I remembered her instructions. I handled the situation by responding in a polite manner to yelling and anger, and consequently it helped me defuse a charged situation, saving me from unwanted embarrassment. I was happy for myself because I was able to deal with situations in a calm manner.

All this happened because I transformed harsh statements into soft statements and it worked pretty well. If you want to skilfully handle charged situations, you should be able to soften somewhat harsh words and tune them to normal. For this purpose, you will have to bring some changes to your personality. The first is to admit that your approach was wrong. I admitted to the lady that I had done wrong by breaking the line, and I should not have done that. The admission of doing wrong melts the hearts of people who even have a heart like a rock. The second and the final change is to submit to accountability. In my case, I was accountable to my wife whom I had empowered to snub me and chastise me whenever I got off the right track. (Mobley, 2014)

Let's take a look at some common examples of softening harsh statements into soft ones. Often, companies use the word downsizing instead of laying off when they are wrapping up their man power. In this way loss of jobs doesn't sound negative. This technique is known as euphemism in English literature. English novelists were fond of using this technique.

Finance companies nowadays use the following words when they are revealing their forecast for the next few months. Their director may say that they had reduced the forecast for the second quarter, but the word 'reduce' sounds negative and it will leave a negative effect on the stock market. Instead, they say that they had adjusted the forecast for the second quarter.

Instead of saying that the company has decided to cut salaries by 2%, they would say that the company has decided to cut down costs or control expenditures. These kinds of softening statements help business improve their image. Better for their business! Softening statements are like a magic spell as they calm down hyper sentiments and anger and project a positive image of an individual and a company.

They are often used in the stock market business. Investors and traders use the word 'negative sentiments' when the stock market nosedives. Apart from that when a particular stock is lagging behind the others, they say that the stock is going through corrections after a rally instead of saying that the stocking is shedding value or is coming down the hill. If you take a look around certain business campaigns and news, you will get to know that business across the word vigorously follow this technique.

Chapter 3: How to Influence People

The world is a complex place to live in and survive. Only the fittest can survive and nowadays being fit means being able to wield a massive influence over people so that people are ready to listen to you and forgive your wrongdoings. If you are a manufacturer, you cannot sell a product unless you learn the trick to influence people and change their minds.

In this chapter I will explain how you can be able to influence people and what its benefits are. You will learn about a number of methods that can be used to shape the opinion of others in your favor.

Brainwashing

Brainwashing is often referred to as a thought reforming and a well-planned technique to influence a person's behavior, beliefs and political opinion. The term has its origin in the United States, surfacing in the military circles when a big number of American military prisoners defected to the communists after getting captured by the Korean military. The soldiers were returned to the United States but the military high-ups were alarmed to learn that the American soldiers were not thinking and acting the same way as they had been trained. A few of them had been harboring anti-America doctrines and had been appreciating the Marx methods to rule over a nation. It all happened during their incarceration period. Experts found out later on that the soldiers were subjected to sleep deprivation and psychological manipulation that are broke down their personality and autonomy.

Nowadays, the United States and other countries who are at war against terrorism believe that the same tactics are applied on the people that are used by religious organizations. We call these people extremists and terrorists. This helps us understand why a sixteen years old teenage girl, who has so much to see and do in life, jumps into a crowd of people and blows herself to pieces in a terrorist attack.

Brainwashing is considered as an invasive form of influence and it demands full isolation which is why it is possible in prisons and in terrorist camps that are mostly isolated from civilized society. It is crucial for the agent to exercise complete control over the target in order to conclude the brainwashing session in a conclusive manner. By complete control, I mean the control over his sleeping patterns, eating schedule, washroom and bathroom needs and any other basic human need such as the need for some fresh air. Once the agent successfully wipes out the data on the brain of the target, he replaces it with a set of beliefs, behaviors of which the target had previously no knowledge.

Some psychologists say that brainwashing is possible under the right conditions while others consider it as a milder form of influence than the media considers it to be. Some definitions of brainwashing demand that the presence of a threat of physical harm is imminent in the brainwashing session while others say that there is a type of brainwashing that don't rely on nonphysical coercion as a means of influence. Experts do believe that the effects of brainwashing to influence others stay for a short span of time. They believe that the popular belief that the target loses his unique identity when he embraces the new planted identity is not right as his true identity is not completely lost but is pushed down into hiding inside the brain. Once the agent stops reinforcing the new identity, the target will recover his old behavior and beliefs. So the verdict is that the agent must reinforce the new identity of the target in a regular manner. (Layton, n.d)

Influence People

You have influence power so do everybody else has. It is the ability to motivate as well as inspire the masses to take action. The power of influence is what makes you stand out among the rest of the lot. This is the major difference between a leader and a manager. Influence, in general, refers to one's ability to exert a positive effect on others in order to convince others to gain support. When you are able to exert influence on other people, you get the power to persuade them and engage them toward an idea.

It is the application of power for gaining the results that you want or to achieve certain objectives for yourself or for an organization. Experts believe that people try to use some key techniques such as logical reasoning, socializing, exchanging, consulting, building alliances and modeling. At the same time there are some dark sides of influencing others such as intimidating, avoiding, manipulating and threatening.

Experts also believe that influence is not an easy feat to pull off. We exercise influence over our kids, partners, and friends and at a bigger level, countries exercise influence power over other nations. The power to influence others is always inside us. All we need is to unleash its potential and reap its benefits. It is a fact that we need a little bit of polishing. Whenever we attempt to affect how most people think and behave or make a decision, we are exercising our power to influence them. Similarly, a smile and even a simple handshake help us socialize with people and influence their opinion. Whenever we break down barriers with strangers, we get into a position to influence them. If you want to know whether people are getting influenced by you or not, you should see if they like you and your thoughts. If they do, they have already been influenced by you. All you need is to kick off the process and get it going. Gradually, you will realize that they wouldn't be able to say 'no' to your requests.

The top rational approach to influencing people is logical persuasion of other people. You should use logic to explain what you need to believe and what you want others to believe. People sometimes are greatly attracted toward logical persuasion. You should tell them what you think about a particular business or an idea. When you communicate with them, they get a chance to your opinion and your thought process. That's how they are likely to appreciate your thoughts, and when they do that, you have got the power to influence them. They will listen to what you say and very possibly do what you want them to do.

Socialization is another tool that is brilliant when it comes to influencing others. By socializing with different people, we get a chance to be open as well as friendly with them. We can talk about their achievements and appreciate them. We can also appreciate their thoughts and opinions that allows us to bring them into our friend circle. The trick is a simple one. We should keep in mind that every person on the planet loves to hear his reasonable praise that's why when we are appreciating someone for a reason, we get great influence over them, which we can use later on.

Another popular technique that we normally use is asking questions from people when we are trying to initiate a project or launching a scheme for our business. Engaging others into giving their input is a brilliant way to bring them into your magical circle of influence. People love when you give them importance and request them to leave their input for your projects. They like to express their opinion on the pros and cons of a particular scheme and how it will affect your business. If you ask them to pass a review on your business project, they will appreciate you and form a positive image of you in their brains. That's where your power to influence them starts. They will listen to whatever you say.

The power to influence can be lethal in the hands of manipulators. Manipulators also use some common but dark techniques to negatively influence others. They will force others to act against their best interests. To accomplish this objective, they will avoid their responsibility and put it on the shoulders of other people. They can use deceit and lies to attain their objective. Also, they will be seen disguising their intentions and withholding certain information.

Manipulators also try to impose themselves on other people by forcing them to comply by using loud voice, arrogance, abrasion and insensitivity that is a preferred technique for bullies. The most heinous technique they can use is to threaten other people to harm them in case they are unable to comply. The threats can be the show of weapons or by describing an example of someone who had been subjected to their wrath for non-compliance of their orders. This is the technique that despots and dictators have been rigorously using throughout the history of the world.

The Features That Matter in Strengthening Your Ability to Influence Others

Leaders have a unique ability to influence others. They master the skills that are needed to assume the role of a leader. These abilities include learning agility, the power of communication and self-awareness etc. If you cannot influence others, you cannot make reality what you have envisioned for the world or for those who are around you such as your family and friends. The people who want to lead don't just command over others but they also become inspiration for others. They know the art of persuading others and also encouraging others. They tend to tap the knowledge of a particular group and direct certain individuals toward some lofty goal.

Leaders should build up a politically savvy mindset. They should also build up a special skillset to view politics at a neutral level and as a crucial part of an organization. They must understand how important politics is for the health of an organization. They should do proper networking to develop their social capital that must include a special mingling strategy. Leaders should think before they respond to people, and also set goals before you decide how to express yourself. In addition, leaders should pay close attention to active listening.

Another important feature of the personality of leaders is that they maintain a robust foundation of trust among employees or followers. Leaders should learn to trust first and then demand the same from their followers or employees in an organization. That's how they are able to convince people to comply with what they say and what they demand. Trust is vital for the growth of an organization, and it helps deal with the toughest of challenges in a fruitful way.

Reciprocity

Let's start this section by understanding the principle of reciprocity. I'll go over the norms of reciprocity and how they can be utilized for powerful influence. I'll show you how to think about applying reciprocity to your own attempts to influence people.

The principle of reciprocity is the basic of foundation of a relationship. It can be defined as one of the most crucial human needs to give back something they have received from the other end of the relationship. When I was a kid, my friend gifted me an expensive fountain pen on my fifteenth birthday, a couple of days before the party. I wasn't used to receiving expensive gifts from friends in that way, but I was really happy because nothing in the list of my birthday gifts even came close to its lush and glamor. It was simply brilliant. The friend was so selfless that he even didn't show up at the birthday party so that I might not remain under his influence because of the gift he had given to me. The birthday cake was cut and the night had gone, but I couldn't forget that pen. I had a powerful urge to return something to him before I started using the pen, and I did exactly that. I didn't use that pen until I gifted him an equally expensive wrist watch. It is human nature that whenever we receive something from person who doesn't had given it without expecting anything in return, the urge in us to return the favor gets the strongest.

If you take a closer look at the world around you, the world is full of reciprocities. When someone takes a favor from his colleague, he returns it with a thank you. The communication doesn't stop there. The person who receives it, returns the favor with a welcome, and it happens on a daily basis. Our brain is naturally wired to return something in exchange for what we receive. Just imagine a girl who has been receiving gifts from her girlfriend for one year but has not reciprocated the favors. Will they friendship last till the end of the world? It is hardly likely that it will. Only the relationships that are built on the principles of reciprocity tend to last for a while. Also, they last until the principle of reciprocity is violated. The same principle works between a buyer and a seller.

You can integrate the principle of reciprocity into your personality and it will help you maintain a healthy and powerful influence over other people. The best strategy is to give something to others without expecting anything in return from them such as a discount and a bonus. If you are businessman and sell a product, you will be able to double up your customer base by using this method. You can offer some gift or some other incentive such as a 'buy one get one free' thing on your product. Also, in return of the package or the favor, ask the customers to leave an email or a message on social media in praise of the products or services of your company. You can offer them access to emails, social media groups or any other forum where they can easily leave their feedback.

You can also thank your customer in reciprocity when you have sent the order. You should take up a personalized approach for thanking your customers. Address them by their name and be specific about the product or service they have requested. Then go on to thanking them from the core of your hearts. That's how you can build a positive image of your brand and also make yourself highly influential.

The Pre-Giving Technique

Pre-giving is the most basic reciprocity technique, and it involves a very simple way of gaining influence. The basic idea at work behind this technique is that when you give someone a physical gift, you will be able to secure favors from them in return. Your likelihood of exercising healthy influence on them increases. Even if the gift you are giving someone is a small one, you are basically creating an expectation that the other person will reciprocate it and that too with gratitude, just because you have made the first move. That's why pre-giving becomes highly important in terms of exercising influence over other people. It shapes up or positively contributes to our first impression on the other person.

A study was conducted to look into the technique of pre-giving and also judge how effective and beneficial it is. Participants believed that the person with whom they were interacting was just another participant while in reality he was one of the actors that researchers had hired to conduct the study. They were only pretending to be participants. In the middle of the experiment, the actors requested the other participants leave the place for a couple of minutes. When they got back, the experiment continued normally as it was getting on before. Sometimes the actor didn't return empty handed, but he had a pair of Coca Cola bottles in his hand. On entering the room, the actor told the real participant that he had brought the drink for him. So the participant received a gift from the actor just like we exchange gifts in normal days.

When the experiment ended and the two participants, one of them an actor, were packing up to leave the room, the actor told the participant that he had been selling raffle tickets and that if he sold more tickets, he would win a prize. It was like a competition so the actor asked the participant if he would buy any tickets. The researchers wanted to check the reaction of the participants.

When the results were prepared and unfolded for the public, it turned out that usually a person is willing to buy just one ticket, but the participants of the study were willing to buy two tickets on average. That was an amazing turn of events. They agreed to pay double price just because they had received a gift in the form of soda from the actor. This showed when someone gives a gift no matter how humble it is in terms of value, we are highly likely to follow his directions. This is a spontaneous reaction which sometimes we cannot explain. Reciprocity principle immediately gets into action when the person demands something from us.

There are certain elements that are crucial for the functioning of the pre-giving technique. It must be kept in mind the time span between these two things should not be extraordinary long. The shorter the time span is, the higher will the compliance level from the other person. The study showed that after the week had passed, the results were slightly different, but a month, the results had totally changed. The effect of the gift and the influence it had brought to the giver had gone into thin air. There wasn't much effect on the participant.

We can give an absolutely free gift just like the one that actors in the above mentioned experiment did. It can be a physical and a free gift. It can be in the form of free content that you offer to your customers in the form of blog posts or eBooks or email letters. When you are providing them useful information for free, you are actually making them feel indebted to you. Another method is to send wish cards to your customers to special occasions such as Christmas or New Year. All the things have the sole objective to give away something absolutely free to your customers or the people around you. The pre-giving technique turns out to be pretty much helpful in business. The key is to give away a gift then ask them for a favor in a short window of time. The favor should be a reasonable one and something that the customers can easily do. (Reciprocity technique #1: pre-giving, n.d)

An Overview of Common Persuasion Techniques

Persuasion can turn out to be a Herculean task if you don't do it right or you don't tread the right path. Convincing a single person on your viewpoint is pretty tough. Just imagine convincing a dozen or a group of fifty people. Still, there are lots of people around us who are pretty expert at convincing others, and they always leave us wondering why it happens that some people have a better ability. Have you ever met a salesman of any company? Some of them are pretty good at cracking a deal with a customer. Convincing others is their bread and butter. They have that steel confidence in their personality that they will be able to convince the people they met to sell things. Psychologists have successfully crafted certain techniques which you can use to boost up your convincing power. Let's review those techniques.

The That's Not All Technique

Although an influence tactic in the "reciprocity" family yet the That's Not All technique takes a different approach to utilizing this principle. Marketers use this technique for persuading potential customers who are still thinking about what to buy from the market. This is a special technique because of the fact that it takes into account making a request and afterwards putting great emphasis on the benefits of the product or service with the help of additional arguments before you ask the person to comply with your request. For example, your salesman is selling motorbikes at a showroom. The hall has been filled with around one hundred customers who are here to buy motorbikes. The showroom has five other companies that have put their products on display. All of them have salesperson who are actively working to sell maximum items. Your salesperson tells the customers about the benefits of buying the motorbike such as great speed, economical average with respect to consumption of oil and lots of other benefits. There is one rider who is demonstrating how the motorbike runs and how it sounds. Just before your salesman makes the call to action, he adds, "That's not all. When you buy the motorbike, you will get ten liters of gas as bonus." (Common Strategies: Common Persuasion Techniques, n.d)

Ten liters of gas is just peanuts in front of a bike that is worth several thousand dollars but the impact it makes on the minds of buyers is huge. It is a free gift from you for them. It will add great strength to your persuasive arguments.

Foot-in-the-Door Technique

The foot-in-the-door technique is a genius application of consistency norms to maximize the chances that someone will agree to do something for you. It's not as violent as it sounds--I promise! This technique involves making a little request that a person is likely to agree upon. When he agrees on the little request, you can go on to make a larger request. You can understand this by the name of the technique. When you are able to step a foot in the door, you are ready to walk through the other doors. When the buyer agrees to your first request, you can secure the right to make them agree to the second favor. Sales personnel use this technique to boost up sales. For example, the salesman for your motor bikes may ask a random customer, "Do you mind telling me which company's motorbikes you ride?" (Common Strategies: Common Persuasion Techniques, n.d)

The customer will think that he is doing a favor to the salesperson by just telling him the name of the company. He will be interested in the question thinking that the workers are doing a kind of survey to collect data about the people who are bike riders. Bike riders usually love to answer questions about their bikes.

Once the first question gets an answer, the salesman can go on to ask the next question.

"Why don't you try our bikes? They are a good ride as compared to your current bike?"

Starting a conversation in this way helps you secure more clients than directly asking them to buy your product or switch to your service. A number of studies have supported this technique as the best technique for salespersons to sell different products. First make a small request and then deciding upon the response of the customer, go on to ask for a bigger favor. This strategy can be applied to any household item such as soap products, electronic devices etc.

Door-In-The-Face Technique

In one last instance of reciprocity in action, the "door-in-the-face" technique takes yet another perspective on how to take advantage of reciprocity norms. This technique is just another method to make a request that tends to operate in the back way. Using this technique, you can make an unreasonable request that the other person is going to refuse right away. This method is quite beneficial in sales negotiations. For example, a motorbike salesman, may offer a customer to trade his old bike for a new one from your company by offering the customer a tiny amount for his old bike. We know the result of this request. The customer is going to refuse it anyway as it was intended by your salesman. When he has received the refusal from the customer, he will then turn toward the customer once again and come back with another offer that is more reasonable than the last one, and that he thinks the customer will incline towards. Even if the second offer is going to be lower than what ought to be reasonable, the customer is going to accept it because he has already been subjected to a ridiculously low offer. (Common Strategies: Common Persuasion Techniques, n.d)

Experts explain that one reason behind the influence of the door-in-the-face technique is that it plays on the sense of guilt of the customer. They realize that they had already declined the initial request of the salesman that's why they should accept the second request. The sense of guilt starts getting over their nerves that they have not helped out the salesman upon the first request. When the second request is made and it also appears to be more reasonable than the first, the customer readily agrees to it. The second request offers them an opportunity to decrease the level of guilt that the customer had experienced.

There is another explanation why this technique worked, and that is the refusal of the customer to the first request gives birth to a grave concern on the part of the customer that his reputation has been torn apart. They may feel that the salesman considered them as uncharitable or somewhat rude or even uncooperative. Let me explain this in simple words. As human beings we are always looking out for a second opportunity whenever we do something wrong. The second request by the salesman turned out to be that second opportunity that the customer had been thinking about. He grabs it and satisfies himself by presenting himself as a fair person. (Common Strategies: Common Persuasion Techniques, n.d)

Low-balling

The low-ball technique is one more way of utilizing the consistency principle to maximize your influence. Using this technique involves being careful about how you present all the necessary information. The low-ball technique is about making a request to the customer and then gaining an agreement on the same from him. You have to change the terms of that deal at the nick of the time. This is an unethical method of securing agreement from the customer, but that's the way to do that.

Take the example of a motorbike salesman who may tell his customer that he is selling a bike for $15,000. The customer happily agrees to pay the price, thinking that he has received the best deal for the bike. Everything is agreed upon. The time comes to sign the agreement papers. It is then that the salesman reveals that the price he told the customer was incorrect, and now he could only sell the motorbike at $18,000. The customer had been waiting for a long time in your office, during which he has made up his mind to purchase the motorbike. That's why he agrees to buy the motorbike at a higher price. This technique also is about saving your reputation in front of the salesman and the other staff. (Common Strategies: Common Persuasion Techniques, n.d)

Consistency

The principle of consistency can be explained from the fact that people, in general, desire to be consistent in words and deeds. Can you recall an event when you had made commitment to a person but could not fulfill it? Did it make you feel good or was it a terrible experience? Most if the people consider it a bad experience. They think it is embarrassing and shameful to leave a commitment in the middle.

People, usually, are highly likely to do things in which they feel more consistent with. They adopt the attitude that they most of the time carry and feel comfortable with. Consistency is considered as an adaptive behavior that really helps when we are trying to influence others. The world is really a complex web in which only the person, who has made up habit to make decisions and do certain acts on a set pattern following a set of values, can survive.

People feel bad if they say that they will do a thing and then change their mind and say that they cannot do that. This inconsistency is also considered as an emblem of unreliability. We tend to struggle for consistency in the commitments we make. We have to keep up with our values and attitudes when we are faced with acting on some plan of action. We have to keep up with our attitudes that we have trained over the past several years.

It is human tendency to not only be consistent in reality but also be able to portray himself as a consistent person. You can do that by making public what you do. You can also talk about it in your family and friend circles. Share it with your partner and friends in addition to mentioning it in your social networks. It works two ways. When people know about our habit of being consistent, they create a sort of pressure that keeps us moving with the same level of consistency. The second benefit is that it portrays our image as a person who doesn't compromise over his principles. It will definitely add to your power to influence people. When you say something, people will be expecting that you will stand by it and that's why they will listen to you and act on what you say.

Chapter 4: Introduction to Social Validation, Liking and Scarcity

In this chapter, I'll cover the basics of social validation, including its relationship with conformity and the way psychologists have understood its effects. Social validation is the greatest way to motivate people. Let me deal with this concept by explaining what symptoms to watch for when you are seeking social validation. Each of us has to go through a certain time when we are subjected to a unique environment due to one or another reason. Sometimes it is because of our new job in a different than in which we have been living. Sometimes it is because of our studies when we have to live in a different city or country to attend a university.

If you have been subjected to a new environment, the chances are high that you might have observed what people do around you. Whenever you meet a stranger, you try to mimic their gestures and language to blend in the environment. This is our first attempt to seek social validation in a totally new place. We just don't want anyone to stare at us and call us a stranger or check our behavior.

If you look at social validation through the lens of psychology, it means that a person is conforming to a social group and also following actions of that particular group to blend in their company or simply to win their trust. Social validation is about adjusting your gestures, language and appearance in accordance with where you are going to or where you are living in. The phrase, When in Rome, do as the Romans do, can explain how social validation works.

Social validation is all about conforming to the traditions of the current environment that you are living in. Adaptation to an alien setting is a natural process and we unintentionally do it sometimes.

Social validation follows the principle of conformity. When a customer is not sure if he should go ahead and buy something, he has to rely on the reviews that other users have made on the benefits of the product. Only after that they are convinced that they reviews are great, the chances of their making the purchase considerably increase. Social validation works on the principle of liking and conformity by a great number of others customers.

Consumers are more likely to buy a product that their peers endorse to them rather than going for the product that celebrities endorse. Consumers are more likely a buy a product from Amazon if it has a good number of positive views.

The "Social Proof" Technique

This theory was first advocated by Robert Cialdini who maintains that a person who is unaware who to behave in a certain social circle, will look forward to other people. Social proof is something that help us discern what is right from the eyes of the other people. what other thinks correct becomes right in our eyes.

When we cannot judge a situation ourselves, we look out for social proof to validate our judgment. Social proof reinforces our judgment or totally reshapes it as well. Social proof works well during the time of crisis when we don't have sufficient time to think and make a decision. Social proof shapes our behavior and the theory that explores and confirms this notion is known as the Informational Social Influence Theory.

Applying social validation to the compelling influence is pretty straightforward. I'll give you some specific mechanisms of how social proof can be used and why it's so effective.

The first mechanisms is uncertainty. It is the fuel that tends to fire up and also feed the mechanisms of social proof. When we face an unfamiliar situation, we become uncertain about the result of the circumstances, that's why we feel the need to refer to our social circle for guidance on the matter. It is a kind of reassurance that we are doing the right thing.

Another mechanism is similarity that tends to motivate us and also enhance our social proof. When we identify ourselves with a group of people, we are highly likely to attend to their recommendations and suggestions. The similarity can be based on age, color, race, nationality, language, physical appearance or some job occupation. Studies suggest that we are more likely to follow the guidelines laid down by our peers with whom we share a similarity.

Social proof helps us move around our social circles without any fear of rejection or odd behavior on part of our peers. We can protect ourselves from taking actions that would make us feel alienated from the society. When a company sells a toothpaste, it includes a tagline that four out of five doctors have recommended it use. That's how they try to validate that our peers have confirmed the use of a particular toothpaste. Testimonials by someone from our social circle are more likely to click our minds than endorsement by celebrities.

There are some dangers of social proof as well, and they can be quite detrimental and hazardous. For example what our peers are doing is not the right thing. If we follow them blindly, we are going to land ourselves in great trouble. Social proof is considered as the most powerful weapon to persuade and influence people. If we use it in the right way, we can be able to improve our personal lives and social interactions.

Liking

Why do companies hire sexy models to sell cars, energy drinks and perfumes despite the fact that it is the males who are greatly attracted toward sport cars and energy drinks? Liking is important when it comes to exercising influence over people. Customers want a website to look good to convince themselves that it is credible and likable. It should have a brilliant design and unique functions that must offer users enjoyment during the time they have to click all the buttons.

If you take a look at the website of Black Clothing, they are hardly using any high quality photos for the visitors to soothe their eyes. Instead they have uploaded a fun video at the start of the website. Users watch this video and enjoy the introduction before they enter the website and explore its pages. The video features multiple hot and beautiful models who are wearing Black Milk Clothes, and are having fun as the preparations for Christmas go on. Liking can be a powerful influence strategy. I'll further show you exactly what I mean by "liking" and why it can be such an important tool of influence. The customers who happened to like the video, are more likely to buy the products from the online store. So physical attraction does wonders when we are trying to get people to like something we want them to.

One especially useful tool for increasing your likability and aiding in your influence attempts is the similarity technique. I'll show you a few examples of this technique in action and also show you how to think about applying this strategy yourself.

This is the second principle of liking. Most of the brands that are being produced across the world fail to relate to the customers. We prefer to purchase things from a company that loves to interact with its customers and is quite empathic. When a corporation gets involved in live interaction with people, people start liking it and its products because they try to find a relationship with the company and the product. For example, Ufone, a cellular company, has created a logo Ufamily. The users of the company now boast of being a part of the Ufamily. They have found a relationship to nurture and take care of. They buy its products because the company has offered them a new identity. They like their slogan and that's why they buy their services.

Nowadays big brands are working hard to cut down on the distance that exists between the customer and the company. They have started to realize that they cannot behave like an alien or a superior being who have the responsibility to provide the customers what they cannot produce themselves. They know that they have to be a friend of you to sell their product. You have to build a kind of reliability as well as similarity. When you know that your customers can relate to you, you can better understand their problems that they face and then provide solutions in accordance with it.

Yet another tool based on liking is the familiarity tactic. You'll see a few examples of familiarity in action, and I'll also dispel some myths about what has to occur for someone to benefit from "familiarity." By using this technique, you can make a conscious effort to create familiar face prior to making a request.

This strategy results in greater compliance in response to the request that you make. People are highly likely to get influenced by the ones they are more familiar with. How to create a sense of familiarity among the people is a challenge that you have to take up.

Introduction to Authority's Influence

It should come as no surprise that authority figures have huge influence. But why? And how deep does that influence run? Influence largely happens when a person or a specific group tends to affect some other person or a group. Power is the capacity of a person or a group of people to influence other people or groups. On the other hand, authority is an offshoot of power that is given in the hands of a specific individual group.

There are number of people who surround us all the time. Among them are religious leaders, doctors, teachers, police, military men and fire fighters. They are people who are in the positions of authority. They are highly revered by the masses because by nature human beings respect authority and power. When a doctor says that we should be consuming sugar, we refrain from it. When a doctor asks us to take medicine for two weeks, we abide by him because we respect what he says. Similarly, when a cop asks us to get out of the car, we respect what he says because of his authority. When a professor of a university asks us to consult a specific book, we go to the market to buy that because we respect his knowledge.

The point is that we like to rely on people whom we consider as having superior knowledge in a particular area such as a medicine, health, teaching, law or other specialized fields. People across the world get easily swayed by the influence of those who are at the helm of affairs. If you are running a business and a staff of fifty is working under your control, you are an authority figure for them. Leaders and manager must understand the principle of authority as it has turned out to be a powerful tool for exercising influences over people.

Where authority is easy to exercise, it also is easier to abuse. It is important you use it in a measured way so that you can be able to maintain your trust among employees. Once you lose the trust among the people who are under your authority, it is nearly impossible to rebuild the same. When you start exercising authority over the people, the other principles of persuasion become easier to implement. An important thing on authority is that you should not be using it for personal gain. If you do that, you will have to pay for it. You will be held accountable for that. You have to use this principle wisely and you will be happier than ever and will be able to bring about more productivity for your firm. To exercise authority over people, you have to take care of the following principles. Let's talk about them one by one.

The very first principle is of aestheticism. You have to present yourself as the one who is immensely careful of his aestheticism. How you present yourself to others is important when you are an authority figure. It has a deep impact on your staff or employees. You have to be able to look like an authority. For example, you should wear an expensive dress suit with a tie that should have a neat knot. Look like an authority figure if you want to be one.

Also, you should buy an expensive sports car that communicate to the onlookers that you possess a high status. If you cannot buy a super costly car, you should keep your old and cheap car well attended. It should be spotless and well-maintained. Always do your hair and don't forget to pay attention to self-hygiene. In short, they should be inspired by your look, and in this way they will be more ready to follow your lead. That's the way human brains are wired. Another aspect of aesthetics is that they boost up your confidence.

You have to remain engaged to exercise your authority especially on new hires in your organizations and new employees in your company. These new entrants will turn out to be a fresh start for you as a leader. You should personally help them so they can navigate through the company and absorb key information that you want them to. You should make sure that they are getting access to all the information you want them to absorb. Also, help the fresh hires to absorb themselves in the culture of your company. Also, communicate the mission, values and vision of your company to the fresh hires along with the 'why' factor behind those values and the vision. You need to welcome them in a way that shows that you are extremely excited for them to join your company.

Remember that if you want to influence people with your authority, you should walk your talk. People start getting annoyed from a person who fails to walk his talk. You need to lead by example. If you want your employees to work from 9 to 5 without a break, you should show them that it is possible by doing them yourselves. If you don't like your staff to wear jeans at the office, stop wearing them yourself.

Last but not least is that you should highlight the achievements of your employees before the other staff members. We love attention, appreciation and a round of applause. This will encourage other employees to follow in the footsteps of the high achiever. In addition, it will boost up their confidence in you as a leader. They will respect you more than ever for respecting people who work hard. It is like the reciprocity principle in terms of appreciation and respect. (Eisenhauer, n.d)

Introduction to Scarcity

Yet another influence principle is that of scarcity. I'll review the nature of this influence principle and why it does what it does. The persuasive power behind making something scarce or limited to attain is quite powerful.

The "Limited Number" Technique

One application of scarcity that you've probably seen a million times is the limited number technique. I'll review a classic study from the science of influence to discover a few refinements of the basics of limited numbers. Cialdini identified that scarcity are among the top six social influence principles that are used to elicit compliance, choice and agreement. Burger and Caldwell conducted a study to assess the impact of the principle of scarcity. They invited some participants for an experiment by making them believe that their personality test scores had been rare. They told them that they fall into the category of the top ten percent. Other participants were told that their scores were more common. The remaining participants believed that the opportunity was unique and scarce so they were more likely to show up and participate in the exercise to make it to the ten percent. In general, research alludes to creating shorting of something in terms of numbers. Just as we saw that participants came again and again in droves to be a part of a bunch of people. The scarcity of the group madly pulled them. One of the many people to make people think is that the quantity of something is reducing. When people are convinced that the number of slots or items are limited, they will be attracted toward it. (Nicholson, 2018)

High Demand

The second principle is creating a high demand. If they perceive that the demand of something is high, they move toward attaining it. In order to elicit scarcity, you need to make sure that the thing is in high demand. For example, avocado remains in high demand in the sub-continent which makes it more desirable and precious. Now apply the same principle to humans. You should develop certain habits and collect such knowledge that people are always willing to listen to you. You should also invest in yourself in terms of training so that people seek after you to gain something useful for their professional life and tips to solve their work-related issues. A person who has 100,000 followers who are ready to listen to his words is considered as highly influential. That's the reason people who have a following on Twitter, Instagram or YouTube are considered as influential. Remaining in high demand is the key to wield a powerful influence over people.

The "Deadline" Technique

Another scarcity tactic is to employ a deadline. You know this one well--or do you? It turns out that the deadline tactic isn't all it's cracked up to be, and I'll show you when this strategy can actually backfire. You can make a choice scarce by setting a time limit around it. You can put an arbitrary deadline on the option and ask people to go for it. This technique can really backfire because humans don't like restrictions. They love to be free that's why they are more comfortable in open scenarios in which they have free time to ponder over something and make a decision accordingly. If the deadline is too short, most people will fail to act thinking that they are busy and they have been subjected to injustice by being offered a short deadline. If you must set a deadline, you should create a strong call to action and keep repeating it in the ears of your customers so that they pay heed to it. One of the best call to action can be: start acting now before time runs out. (Nicholson, 2018)

Chapter 5: How to Talk

This chapter will show you how you can improve your speech that could make an impact on the masses. You will learn about certain words that you must include in your speech, words that you should do away with and techniques to use hypnotic language. You will also learn how to master hypnotic language and how you can use your body language to increase your circle of influence.

The chapter contains discussions on the Zeigarnik Effect, the Yes ladder, probing questions and pattern interrupt. You will be able to tune your speech to make it more effective and full of power.

Words to Use

Experts say that the biggest problem of the world is that we cannot persuade people to do what we want them to. We always have to confront defiance and most of the time, defiance wins. If we want to influence others and motivate them to do something, we have to convey our message in the right words. This brings us to choosing the right words to communicate our thoughts and desires. It is not just necessary for persuading people for a short while, but this ability to persuade others is also necessary for building up a good leadership quality. It demands certain stellar communication skills and also has the ability to boost up human connection. Let's go through a rundown of some magic words that can do a tremendous job while we are communicating to others.

The first word is 'Yes.' This word is a part of a lot of languages other than English. What is at the top of the fears that lots of people across the world harbor? It is the fear of facing rejection that keeps us. Our brain is wired to link the word 'no' to rejection, and that's what our brain doesn't accept. This means that the word 'yes' has a totally opposite effect on our brain. 'Yes' is perceived by our brain as a positive word and a sign of mutual understanding. If you use this word more often in your communication, you will be able to connect to the positive part of the brains of your listeners. This works perfectly well if you apply this technique on your marketing campaign. Your customer wants to be accepted by you. By hearing a streak of 'yeses,' they will be able to ease out the tension that is accumulated in their brains. Studies suggest that you should incorporate at least three yeses into your speech to make your speech effective.

The second most important word in your speech should be their name. When you call someone by their name, it means you appreciate them and value them in your life. It is the best way to win someone and bring her on your side. A person's name is the sweetest sound he can ever hear.

The most important word among all is the word thanks. Gratitude is always the most appreciated and sprightly thing that a person can ever hear. If you are running a company, you can show some gratitude to your employees by saying thanks to them for their services. It can be your first step to build a healthy relationship with your team. When the employees feel appreciated, they will be more motivated, and they are more likely to do your job in an efficient and brilliant manner. You should be ready to see considerable improvement in the time they give to your work and the level of quality they used to deliver. Similarly, you can thank your customers for buying your goods or services. The word 'thanks' will make them feel respected, productive, happy and engaged. People take enough rejections in a single day. Amidst this, a 'thanks' from you will be nothing less than a blessing for them. When you say thanks to people, they start appreciation, and the next step after appreciation is respect.

Words Not to Use

The English language contains over a million words in total. Setting aside profane words and slang, you can use all of them in your speech. Still, there are some words that you must avoid in order to successfully influence people. Let's break them down below.

The first word is 'should' which you should avoid to use in your speech. Should reveals certain weaknesses in your personality such as a weak decision making power and an absence of commitment. If you want to show the world that you are a committed person, you cannot use the word 'should.' By not using I mean you should use it where it is crucial to use, and not in any random sentence or phrase.

Another most frequent word that we speak is hope. Hope this happens. Hope that happens. Hope I become a billionaire. If we see the word in an independent position, it has a positive meaning but when we use it in different sentences, it may suggest indecisiveness, desperation and frustration. It may suggest that something is not happening despite your continuous effort. It conveys a sense of indecision. You can replace the word with desire, ambition and goal.

Probing Questions

There are lots of types of probes that you can use. They depend on what you are saying and what you want to discover. Here is a rundown different probing questions. Some probing questions are asked for a clarification. Sometimes a speaker speaks vaguely or in an extremely unclear language that needs clarification. See the following questions.

- What did you mean by that?

- What would you be doing in the coming week?

- Would you mind telling me something about this product?

Sometimes a speaker has concluded a session or is taking time to breathe for a while, and you are confused whether to walk away or to wait for them to start speaking for their second session.

- Is there anything you want to explain?

- Is that all?

- Have we reached the end of the session?

Zeigarnik Effect

If you have been a student or are a student, you can tell that your experience of revising exams might explain that concentration has the power to help you better remember certain pieces of information. Students get involved in cramming lots of knowledge and rigorous sessions of physical exercise. They will also be ready for taking a mock test before sitting in the real exam.

Up till now interruption during our work or study was considered as a bane for our work or study, but now studies have found that interruption can improve our focus and also our memory of the lesson that we were reading while we were interrupted. It was first discovered by a Lithuanian based scientist whose name was Bluma Zeigarnik. He experimented on the effect of observation and how does it get affected by certain changes and conditions of our brain. He conducted a study by which he found out that the faster a task stands completed, the least we will remember it. They linked forgetting of something to its completion in the brain. Incomplete tasks tend to stay in our brain for a longer time because our brain keeps reminding us that something is incomplete and demands our attention. For example, we remember what books we have to read and what notes we have to consult until we are done with the examination. (The Zeigarnik Effect Explained, n.d)

Zeigarnik did a number of experiment on different participants and later on found that the participants, who were interrupted during task, showed a 90% improvement in recalling things. The result suggests that when we desire a task to be finishes soon, we will remember it until we have completed it. Until we actively rehearse it, we will definitely forget it over time. (The Zeigarnik Effect Explained, n.d)

Pattern Interrupt

A pattern interrupt is used to switch the other person's strategy. All of us have patterns of behavior that have been made of the sequences of our habits. Habits affect us as an individual and also as a leader. All people have some kind of habit that they want to change. We have to do lot of things on a daily basis and these lots of jobs are done smoothly because we practice them each day. These automated habits that are an important part of our brain out of subconscious mind and the muscle memory. These habits rule over our lives. These tasks include driving a bike, drinking water, wearing clothes and combing your hair. The memory of the place where you sit to watch the television, the location of the remote control of the television. All these are automated habits. They are quite economical for us because we things start happening automatically, and they don't stress our thinking power that tends to free our mind of the burden of many things. When the brain is less engaged, it makes fast and efficient decisions.

Yes Ladder

If you take a closer look at people, you will know that each of them has created a predictable pattern to follow. If you understand them, you can use them to boost up sales revenues. This principle suggests that we have to be consistent when it comes to our attitudes and actions. The Yes ladder is considered as a top persuasion method that is aimed at getting the customer to say yes to the question that you have crafted for them. They can also say yes to a specific situation such as making a sales pitch or organizing a meeting with the customer. The process demands that you create a series of questions that would start in a trivial way but lose their triviality as you keep on asking more questions. Each of the subsequent question that they answer is likely to make them comply with the last one. That's how it goes on.

Studies say that it doesn't matter if the questions you are asking are relevant to the sales or not. Let's see how a salesman can create a Yes ladder.

Salesman: What is the name of this street?

Customer: This is Harley Street 113.

Salesman: Is it Woofer Town?

Customer: Yes, you are in Woofer Town.

Salesman: Great! Do you live in this glamorous house?

Customer: Yes, it is my house. Thanks for the compliment.

Salesman: Great! I just wanted to let you know that we are going to give away free estimates for house painting in the area. Can you find some time to come over to the Town Hall late in the afternoon or anytime tomorrow.

Customer: I'll be there tomorrow.

This is how the salesman can build the yes ladder. We have got a couple of yeses before making them agree on the real issue that is to make them willing for a free estimation of how much painting the house will cost. Let's break down the yes ladder into steps.

The first step is to identify what is going to be the big yes in your communication which in my case has been getting the agreement of the customer on a free estimate for a full house paint. It can be anything else such as sale of a car, sale of full house, sale of cleaning services or pest control services or any other thing.

The next step is building the ladder. Once you have noted down the big yes, you can then take a backward approach and initiate building the further rungs of your yes ladder. In the example, the salesman built the yes ladder by inquiring about the name of the street and the name of the town. Then he went on to get the fourth consecutive yes from the customer on getting a free estimate on how much painting his house would cost. This is a kind of building a yes compliance.

The easiest way to get the first yes to ask a random question that you already know. You have to identify something that you know the answer to. For example, our salesman asked the customer about the name of the street on which he was standing, then he inquired about the name of the town. He was sure that he would get two clear yeses by these questions. This proved to be a lubricant for the engine of our yes ladder. The important point to mention here is that you have to preplan your yes ladder, which mean that you should create questions that would get you the yeses you are looking forward to.

The last step is a bit risky as well. Each question will help you climb up the ladder and get close to your sales objective. You need to keep pushing a little more when you are climbing your way up. Before you go on to take the big risk, you need to exhaust at least three to five attempts. (Greene, 2017)

Hypnotic Language Patterns & Embedded Commands

English language is a very deep language and it has welcomed lots of revisions, grammars and words from other languages. We can structure the thoughts and put together a strong hypnotic language patterns. This may surprise many people that all of us at one time or another use hypnotic language in our day-to-day meet ups. It affects our lives and what also what we hear, see and feel, but sometimes we use it in the wrong way and bring out negative results. In this section I am going to discuss certain hypnotic language patterns you can use for fun, to boost up sales, for direct hypnosis and for seduction. Once you are on your way to understanding the structure, you can create your own pattern of hypnotic language and use it in your speech.

Hypnotic Pacing Statements

If you want to get the brains of the people feeling slippery, you should use some pacing statements. They should be true. Let's take a look at some of the statements.

And just breathe in....

As you hear what I say...

Just listen to what I am saying to you...

Get relaxed in that chair beside the stove...

If you closely observe, all these phrases and sentences have the power to touch the soul of the listener. They immediately grab the attention of the listener.

Subtle Hypnotic Language

Subtle language is considered as a powerful language. Let's see an example of a lawyer who is trying to convince the judge on the innocence of his client. Let's take a look at the following two examples and decide which one is more influential than the other.

I suggest to you that Mr. Adam is innocent.

Respected sir and the members of jury, you listened to the statement of Mr. Adam and examined the evidence. You may take the option that he is innocent in light of the evidence.

Now think which one of the above statements has greater influence than the other one? In the first sentence, the lawyer made a stubborn and lifeless assertion that Mr. Adam was innocent that fell on deaf ears. In the second example, the lawyer tried to recreate the images of Mr. Adam while he made the statement in his defense and also of the evidence that attempted to prove his innocence. The lawyer went into the details to explain his viewpoint to the jury, which helped him make an impact on the minds of the panel.

How to Master Hypnotic Language

Hypnotic language is something that is pretty difficult to master. It is nothing less than a passion to follow. People find themselves behaving as a silly person, but sounding silly is not the only hurdle in their learning process. People know the words and sentences but still they find it hard to practice in front of other people because they feel reluctant to do that. Some of them get nervous while others find it reluctant to utter the words that they are not used to speak otherwise.

The foremost technique to learning hypnotic language is to write it down and practice. Do this every other day and you will find it to be fun and a faster way to learning new skills. Like all the other things, daily practice helps polish hypnotic language. Divide your sessions in short periods with short breaks so that you may not get bored of the work. Feel no pressure and no effort at all. Instead do it in a fun way. Imagine that you are learning a new skill that is going to immensely aid you in your practical life. You need to jot down all the major hypnotic language patterns and then combine them by giving them short time to learn. See the following example.

"And the more you remember the relaxation that's within... that's right... this is just for you... now sit here... I am beginning to wonder... deep inside...from the core of the heart...... the depths of comfort... are yours to explore... so much more of the best of who you've always been... at heart...So much to say..." (Tyrrell, 2014)

Everybody Lives in a Different Reality

Quantum physics says that every one of us sees the truth in a different way, because every one of us creates what they see in their surroundings. The theory suggests that reality is not something that is carved in stone, and it is a pretty complex idea to fully grasp. Quantum physicists as well as meta-physicists have started to explore the idea more deeply than before. Everyone we meet has his own platform that gives them something to stand on. It is just like a moral standpoint that they have belief in. Their beliefs represent who they are and who they want to be as a person.

Some people believe that human race has been degenerating at a fast pace while others believe that if human race is doing pretty well. There is a massive shift in their perspectives. Some people think bumblebees might be the reason behind the food crisis that we are facing today in the world. Another person is of the belief that the problem of bumblebees takes the back seat and it is corruption that is a major issue for the world. This is proof that people are not seeing the same reality. They are living with different versions of reality.

Body Language For Influence

The way most people carry themselves can either help them in their affairs or hinder their progress. Human beings consistently give off signals from bodies all the time, which tells others how to respond to them. It also tells about their mood and character as well. The foremost of all is your smile. It is a robust to connect with the other people. Big smiles help people consider you as a confident and approachable person. People who wear a big smile are considered as warm, approachable and confident. A smile is considered as the gateway to building a strong relationship. People are always willing to help you and listen to you if they like your viewpoint. When you meet someone, it is quite important to wear a smile to look genuine. If you are not in a good mood, it is a good idea to recall a happy memory and produce a genuine smile. If a person you are talking to is not in a good mood, you can gradually develop a smile and win his heart.

When a person has a perfectly good rapport with you, it is quite easy to make them listen to your speech or your point of view. You should match your body movements with theirs. Mimic their movements and it will greatly help you feel involved. For example, when the person pick up a pen, you should pick up one too. If they put their hands on the table, you should do the same. That's how you will be able to secure a place in their hearts.

Conclusion

If I say to my girlfriend, "I like your dress" in a way that I am staring at the sky or my eyes are chasing a couple of rabbits going down the hole, she will be perturbed by the manner in which I said those words. Instead if I wear a smile on my face and make a direct eye contact, she will love it and take it as a compliment. Rolling of eyes, shaking of the head and other such gestures make us feel sarcastic and critical.

If you tend to look directly at the other person whom you are talking to, it will greatly help you communicate your sincerity and also add the flavor of directness to your communication. On the other hand if you look down or away most of the time, you show them lack of confidence. Too much stare at a person will make him feel very much uncomfortable and he will consider it invasive, to say the least, but this doesn't mean that you should break the eye contact. Keep in mind that you need to be relaxed and also keep it steady. Don't look away as it is going to make them uncomfortable.

Our body posture also matters a lot when it comes to influencing others. Solid research has proved that our standing positions, sitting positions and walking postures greatly affect how we make an impact on others. An active and solid posture while someone talks to you is the way to make a mark on the other people. If you are not active and have adopted a passive stance, the other person will be at an advantage. He will have an upper edge during the communication or any business deal you are going to strike.

Gestures are a part of your expression of certain emotions. They tend to accentuate your message to the people. They add emphasis, warmth as well as openness to your style. Gesturing is considered as a cultural behavior.

If your gestures are relaxed and carry meaning, they will inject depth or infuse power to your conversation. Another thing that has a great impact on how you influence others is the distance you keep when you are talking to others. If you are sitting or standing closely to a person, it means that you are very intimate to them with respect to the relationship. Here moderation is the key to success. If you come too close to the other people, you may be on your way to offend them, and they will immediately become defensive. This factor depends on different cultures. In the eastern culture, there is a limit of distance between two people while in the western culture, there is no such limit. It also depends on the mood of the other person. In some cases when you get close to the other person, she may consider it a request to cut down the distance and be intimate with you.

The book has educated you how you can be a better influencer for people. It explained what methods you can use to make other people attracted toward you. It depends on different things such as how you have made your first impression and what elements have you chosen for effective communication. You have learnt the key to influence other people. You have learnt several techniques such as reciprocity, pre-giving technique, consistency and many others. You have also learned what social validation is and how social-proof works.

Influencing is about how you carry yourselves and how your portray yourselves. For example, you should express it what you say by your words. Only then there will be sufficient substance in your message. Have you ever seen someone who is speaking loudly and wearing a smile on his face? The combination is hardly a reality. When we are angry, it is expressed from our words and on the face. You should bring yourself in a certain state of mind and then see how your face looks in the mirror. From there you can calculate what expression should be paired up with what kind of words. Now you can think about something and then match your facial expression with it. This book has equipped you with the techniques and methods you need to be a highly influential person.

About the Author

Jason Miller is a bestselling author and human psychology researcher, a dedicated student of the human condition. Obsessed with self-improvement and fascinated by the power of the mind, his personal mission is to help people realize their full potential and reach higher levels of fulfillment and consciousness.

Jason writes books that focus on changing old habits, overcoming self-destructing behavior and the best strategies on how to deal with rejection. He is based in Los Angeles, California. Jason possesses a BSc in psychology and a graduate degree and has worked with many people from all walks of life.

References

Common Strategies: Common Persuasion Techniques. (n.d). Retrieved from https://www.psychologistworld.com/behavior/compliance/strategies/overview

Eisenhauer, T. .(n.d). How to Use the Persuasion Principle of "Authority" at Work. Retrieved from https://axerosolutions.com/blogs/timeisenhauer/pulse/837/how-to-use-the-persuasion-principle-of-authority-at-work

Green, J. (2017). How to Prime Prospects to Sat "Yes" (and Make the Sale). Retrieved from https://www.phoneburner.com/blog/how-to-prime-prospects-to-say-yes/

Harmer, S. (n.d). 8 Ways To Stop Emotional Manipulation. Retrieved from https://www.lifehack.org/articles/lifestyle/8-ways-stop-emotional-manipulation.html

Layton, J. (n.d). How Brainwashing Works. Retrieved from https://science.howstuffworks.com/life/inside-the-mind/human-brain/brainwashing.htm

Making a Great First Impression. (n.d). Retrieved fromhttps://www.mindtools.com/CommSkll/FirstImpressions.htm

Mobley, C. (2014). Softening the Sharps and tuning up normal. Retrieved from https://purposefulfaith.com/harsh-words/

Nicholson, J. (2018). 4 Ways to Use Scarcity to Persuade and Influence. Retrieved from https://www.psychologytoday.com/us/blog/persuasion-bias-and-choice/201812/4-ways-use-scarcity-persuade-and-influence

Reciprocity technique #1: pre-giving. (n.d). Retrieved

from https://gohighbrow.com/reciprocity-technique-1-pre-giving/

Stillman, J. (n.d). 10 Techniques Used by Manipulators (and How to Fight Them). Retrieved from https://www.inc.com/jessica-stillman/10-popular-techniques-used-by-manipulators-and-how-to-fight-them.html

The Zeigarnik Effect Explained. (n.d). Retrieved from https://www.psychologistworld.com/memory/zeigarnik-effect-interruptions-memory

Tyrrell, M. (2014). Master Hypnotic Language Patterns in 3 Straightforward Steps. Retrieved from https://www.unk.com/blog/3-steps-to-hypnotic-language-mastery/

www.ingramcontent.com/pod-product-compliance
Lightning Source LLC
Chambersburg PA
CBHW060359080526
44583CB00012B/395